The Children of New York City:

Straight from the Heart 2009

Edited by Natalie Mckenzie

Order this book online at www.trafford.com
or email orders@trafford.com

Most Trafford titles are also available at major online book retailers.

Print information available on the last page.

ISBN: 978-1-4269-1300-6 (sc)
ISBN: 978-1-4269-1302-0 (e)

Trafford rev. 10/17/2019

www.trafford.com
North America & international
toll-free: 1 888 232 4444 (USA & Canada)
fax: 812 355 4082

Contents

Contents

Contents

3rd Grade

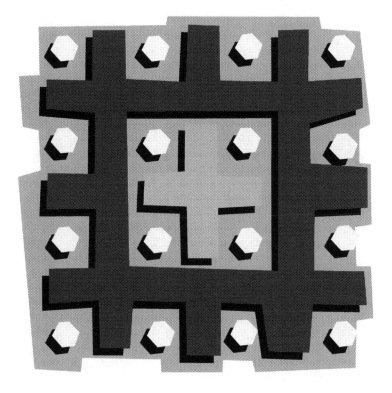

Untitled

By Alana Leitch
Grade 3

Deer are my favorite,
I like them a lot.
They're not to be heard,
They just stay in one spot.
I also like deer
Because they are brown.
They do not act
Like silly clowns.
If I saw one,
I would shout and scream.
But that would just mess up
My beautiful dream.

Untitled

By Margarite Morano
Grade 3

One little flower staring at me.
Sitting there singing and swaying with the breeze.
With the sun above,
And the grass strewn about,
One little flower just hanging out.
With birds flying by and bees buzzing through,
Fall will come as seasons will do.
One little flower sleeping under the snow
Until Spring comes he's laying low.

Lucy

By Gina Garafola
Grade 3

Oh Lucy you're so crazy
Your husband Ricky is kind of lazy.
You have a friend Ethel who's short and frumpy
And her husband Fred who's always grumpy.
The Lucy show has laughing power,
Too bad it's only a half an hour.
Lucy gets into trouble cause she's tricky
She's always calling out for Ricky.
I wish the plot was somewhat juicy.
But anyway I still love Lucy.

November

By Bess Daniel and Ellie Bauer
Grade 3

Orange, red, yellow, brown
All the colors of November
People screaming Fall is here!
It's almost the winter time of year.
Getting darker everyday and night
Feels like it's never going to get bright!

ALL THESE HOLIDAYS ARE COMING!

THANKSGIVING is in sight
But they're no presents at this time.

But a little later
It's CHANUKAH and CHRISTMAS.
All the presents will be
MINE!

Then the NEW YEAR comes
And we welcome 2009!

An Irritating Creature

By Zaharyah Benyisrael
Grade 3

There was an irritating creature

Lying on my mother's bed.

It was hairy, with floppy wings and

Speckled horns of red.

Each time I try to go to bed,

This is what my mother said,

"Arghh! There's a monster on my head!"

I tried to catch him as she screamed,

"Get that monster, I've just cleaned!"

I ran to get it off her head,

And tossed it in the outdoor shed.

I sailed it out to the dark, blue sea,

But it kept coming back to follow me.

By now we are angry, without a doubt;

And that's when we finally figured it out.

We had thought that the creature was simply no good,

But learned it was sweet and just misunderstood.

Untitled

By Mary Navarro
Grade 3

Nature is beauty.

Nature is kind.

Nature is lovely.

Nature is mine.

Rabbits are all these things as well.

They make nature really swell.

They run.

They jump.

They hop.

They bounce.

They can live in a forest or even in my house.

There colors are many.

There sizes are too.

They are all UNIQUE like me and you.

4th Grade

Leaves

By Samantha Kerr
Grade 4

Twirling, swirling
Round and round
As the leaves fall to the ground
Orange, red, yellow, brown

There they go down, down, down
Scarlet, green, tan and gold
What a beautiful thing to behold.

Although I like all types of weather
I prefer the autumn better.

<u>Nature</u>

By Racquel Leonie
Grade 4

The sweet scent of the flowers and
The gentle summer breeze,
The steady sound of the river,
Flowing to the seas,
Remind me of my love for nature,
And how it makes me feel.
I love to hear the birds sing.
Oh what joy they bring.
The whispers of the wind echoing
Through the trees'
The fresh air of the countryside
Is what I love to breathe.
Nature is all around. It is part of me.
Everyday I awake,
It's the first thing that I see!

Ali His Story

By Cheyenne Moody
Grade 4

My name is Cheyenne Moody from Harlem USA,
For Black History Month this is what I have to say:
The person I choose is Muhammad Ali,
He floats like a butterfly and stings like a bee.
You know you can't hit what your eyes can't see,
This brother boxed so viciously.

This is a black man that couldn't be sold,
He went to the Olympics and brought home the gold.
He turned the fight game completely around;
He had to do this to wear the crown.

People came to see him with love and hate,
Then dollars turned to millions
as they rushed through the gate.
He beat Liston, Patterson and even big George,
They all went down in the round he called.
He's the greatest fighter you ever saw,
He slipped, bobbed, and weaved a seamless war.

Now what he did was considered a crime,
He lost three years but never did time.
He let the whole world know how he felt,
And then he came back and regained the belt.
He was the greatest fighter, pound for pound,
Now you tell me just how great that sounds.

Now just when you thought he had the game in order,
Snap, crack, pop out came his daughter.

She had style, grace, and even finesse,
She'll whip anybody when she's at her best.
She showed a great deal of determination,
She be stinging too, Laila, the next generation.

She continued on with the fame and the glory,
Hold up, wait a minute, that's a whole different story.
From Harlem USA, my name is Cheyenne Moody
Now what you've just heard was my story,
About the greatest boxer in history
Goes by the name, Muhammad Ali.

<u>Untitled</u>

By Kayla Persaud
Grade 4

There once was a girl named Jade.
She joined a circus parade.
She dressed as a clown,
And fell purposely down.
And on the floor she just laid.

Autumn Leaves

By Isana Sultan
Grade 4

"Follow me little leaves," said the wind one day,
"Come to the park with me and play.
Put on your coats of yellow, red and gold,
For summer has left and the days are cold."

The little leaves heard the wind's whistling call,
And drifting and fluttering down they fall
Looking pretty in their fine attire,
They danced and flew,
Humming a tune,
For me and you!

Veterans

By Brianna Delacruz
Grade 4

Very Brave
Everyday helping us
Taking chances
Everyone should thank them
Risking their own lives
Allowing us to live free
Nothing can stop them
Sacrificing their lives for our country

Veterans' Poem

By Amanda Clark
Grade 4

You left your beds; you left your homes,
We remember you as the day goes on.

As the war goes on we cry and cheer,
For the war goes on and we're still here.

Our freedom is safe 'cause you fought for us,
The first tear fell
When you when you walked out the door.

One more hug, one more kiss,
Then you must move on.

When you come back from war.
I hear crying, kissing, hugging and more.

There is a big party for your safe return,
We are happy you're finally home.

But we know you will leave again
So we just have to pray on.

There's a Party in the House

By Nichols Benevisto
Grade 4

Mom left me alone
So I wanted to have some fun.
I got out the chips and chocolate
And some bubble gum.

I'll call up some friends,
To get this Party started.
I hope it doesn't happen again
Because last time someone farted.

Now we're cranking up the music
And we're having a blast.
But when I looked at the clock,
I said "OMG," so much time has past.

Now I'm starting to get worried,
It's a very big mess in the house.
But then mom came in
And everyone was as quiet as a mouse.

"Joe what's going on" mom said.
We're uuuummmmm: Having a party,
Am I dead.
No. What? Why?
This party is great
For your little brother is turning eight.
Happy Birthday!
Yaaaaaayyyyy!

My Life

By Josiah Henry
Grade 4

My life is good
My life is bad
Sometimes I'm happy
Sometimes I'm sad

I love my life
And you should too
If you don't
I feel bad for you

When I'm Mad

By Brianna Mays
Grade 4

When I'm mad I do not share
I don't even take a chance to glare

I jump up and down
Don't even touch the ground

My head is gonna burst into flames
For sure I will take the blames

When I am mad I stomp my feet
Then I start to feel more heat

I take three breaths so I don't get sad
And that's what happens when I'm mad

Christmas Time

By Tania Nelzy
Grade 4

Hustle and bustle and hurry and run
Looking for gifts that bring so much fun
A visit to Santa we also must make
The food preparations must get underway
Like cookies and candies for our special day
Gifts must be wrapped and
Bows must be tied
Trees must be trimmed
Lights hang outside
Cards must be bought
Cards must be signed
Addresses are mailed to reach friends on Christmas time

The Beach

By Malik Henderson
Grade 4

When the cold weather is done
I start making my plans
To have fun in the sun.
Playing in the surf and the sand,
My favorite place is the beach.
I go as much as I can;
Swimming and playing around.
Sometimes I even get a tan.
I can't wait for summer.
Man oh Man!
On hot summer days,
At the beach,
Instead of in front of a fan.

Lovely Nature

By Laurisa Peters
Grade 4

The wind
Blows on my skin
The sun
Shines on my head
I see the grass
On my feet
And the Birds
Singing a sweet song.

The moon
Is full
And the stars
Shine bright,
I lay and listen
To the crickets
In the stillness
Of the night.

Then I said
To myself
What a
Beautiful world
And God was right
When He made
Both day
And night

Nature,
Oh how I love you,

I love the wind,
Rain, stars and moon.
Creatures and the sun
God made those things
And it is lots of fun.

My Clubhouse

By Kaelyn Edwards
Grade 4

Hey you!
Yeah you.
Come inside
You'll have a great time.

Here we go!
Walk through the bamboo vines
And we'll have some great times.
We'll sit under a tree,
And hopefully we won't see a bee.

You can think
And have a cold drink.
You can have the snack
That you brought in your sack.

We'll have fun
And there's room for everyone.
So come inside and you decide
If my clubhouse is a good place to hide.

The Baseball Parade

By Vashane Campbell
Grade 4

All the teams lined up,
Like anxious little pups.
With moms and dads in tow,
Up the hill they walked real slow.

Clowns with frowns,
In rainbow colored gowns
Made silly grins,
As they turn and spin.
The middle of the street,
People start to meet.

Oh! What a treat,
To hear the drums beat
Some kids liked walking,
While others enjoyed talking.

The town folks gather around,
As they marched their way
To the playground.
Soon they were at the park,
Someone's dog made a cheerful bark.

Music til after dark,
The baseball parade in the ball park.

BLUE

By Jesse Jacob
Grade 4

Blue is the wings of a dragon.
Blue is the wheels of a wagon.

Blue is the chair in the room.
Blue is the feeling of complete doom.

Blue is the cover of a book.
Blue is the apron of a cook.

Blue is a fuzzy, furry robe.
Blue is the water on the globe.

Blue is the dropping tears of sadness.
Blue is the feeling of anger and madness.

Blue is the slime of a slug.
Blue is the handle of a mug.

Blue is everything in the sky.
Blue is a layer of an eye.

Blue is the heat of a fire.
Blue is the want of pure desire.

Blue is the gem in a ring.
Blue is a song people sing.

Math Monsters

By Paul Fata
Grade 4

Every night I go to sleep,
Math Monsters come out to play with me.
Bursting out of my dream,
Wake me up: **1, 2, 3!**
All I feel is a stinky breeze,
Its because there's a monster on me!
This math monster has **divided** me.
Can you please **add** me up?
I have gotten **subtracted** into little pieces.
They have so many diseases.
I'm fast asleep
They are still nibbling at my feet,
What do you know
They have **multiplied** my feet.
Then I have a dream;
I'm flying high in the sky.
Asleep I'm still on my bed,
Good night,
Sleep tight,
Don't let the Math Monsters
Eat your feet
Because you'll end up like me.

5TH GRADE

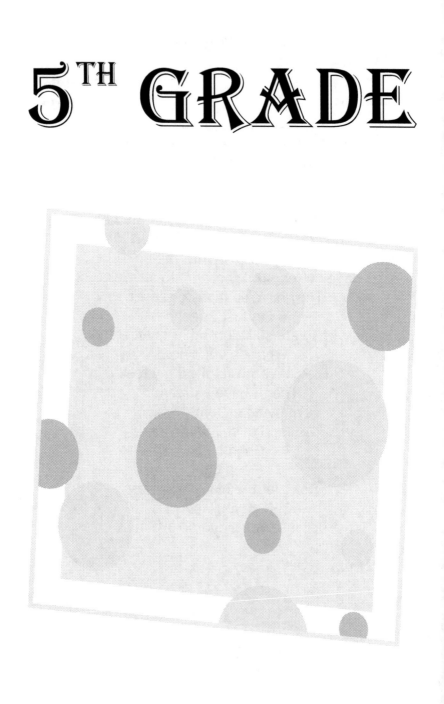

The MATHMETICIAN is on the LOOSE!

By Bharath Ayloo
Grade 5

The mathematician is on the loose!
Addition, multiplication, subtraction, division,
fractions, variables, equal equation
Math is a no brainer to him!

Calculations, computations,
Always reaching expectations!
To him math is such a breeze!
He wants to spread this disease

He has no ordinary brain.
This mathematician is insane.
He spreads math fevers all abut.
While he calculates with no doubt.

Some say his biology is
Chips and technology!
Is this the truth?
This is a warning from me,
Don't under estimate the mathematician
Because it's

ME!

Trees

By Sherman Samuel
Grade 5

Trees are the kindest things I know
They do no harm they simply grow.

And spread a shade for sleepy cows
And gather birds among their own.

They give us fruit and leaves above
And wood to make our houses of.

And leaves to burn on Halloween
And in the spring new bugs of green.

They are first when days began.
To touch the beams of the morning sun.

They are last to hold the light.
When evening changes into night.

And when a moon floats on the sky the
Hums a drowsy lullaby.

Mr. O'Beany

By Jazmine Francis
Grade 5

Hey, I've seen you before
You were at the 99 cents store
Standing with Mr. O'Beany
Who is such a Meany
He never lets you talk
When you walk
He never lets you play
In a parade
He never lets you dance or have fun
Or prance around in the sun
He never lets you sing or eat a lollipop ring
And when you hear a happy tune
His face frowns like a wrinkled old prune
That is all I can say about Mr. O'Beany
He is such a grump, he is such a Meany.

<u>Desk</u>

By Lawrence Ryan
Grade 5

A desk is like a monster

That eats books

Uses pencils as forks

Paper as plates

And pens as spoons.

His favorite treat is homework.

My desk is always messy

Because I'm afraid to clean it

Because if I stick my hand in

He'll probably just eat it.

<u>Math</u>

By Ariel Ocontrillo
Grade 5

Dreadful Division
Magnificent Multiplication
Strong Subtraction
Amusing Addition
Fantastic Fractions
Never quitting Numbers
Entertaining Estimates
Amazing Answers
Powerful Products
Quick Quotients
Demanding Differences
Super Sums
Daring Divisors
Fearless Factors
I love Math!

Smelly Socks

By Darion Hosein
Grade 5

Smelly socks all over the place,
My socks are so vulgar,
They're a **disgrace!!!**

Smelly socks all over the place,
I'm sure they made a movie,
About my smelly socks,
I think it was called **B.O. Rocks!!!**

Smelly socks all over the place,
They'll burn your eyes,
They'll burn your feet,
They'll burn until you look **like dead meat!!!**

Slow Love

Selah Sansculotte
Grade 5

To: Mom

I love the tenderness
When I touch her skin
I love the beautiful body you're in

I love the peach scent
That comes from your head
I love the dimples
On your face that red

I love it when I look at you
And the way you look at me
I will always thank you for creating me.

6th Grade

Do You Care

By Catrina Wiltshire
Grade 6

Do you care about me?
Or am I one of the leaves in any tree?
Don't say you care about me
When you only need me to care for you.
Never say you will be there
When you are far away and I'm here.
Never say you're coming
When away you're always running.
You left me crying many times before,
I cried so hard my body almost collapsed on the floor.
I wanted no part of you
Sometimes I thought I even hated you.
You said you loved me,
But you straight forgot about me.
You're just another bird I swear,
Flying around everywhere.
One day like all birds you must come down
Then we can meet on common ground

THE LEADER

By Bernice White
Grade 6

If only they knew how it is for me
I'm turning 13, the world I begin to see.
My friends began to change right before my eyes,
And now they start telling all sorts of lies
They hang around together in groups of three and fours
The language that they use... isn't gentle anymore
The kids that seem most lonely wind up in packs
And those that stand alone they talk behind their backs
Somehow I feel rejected because I don't conform
Those stepping to their own beat don't seem to be the
norm
I watched a few just fade away, with drugs and alcohol
And many more have given up, too many to recall
Alcohol is an option for everyone in my school
I lost a friend to booze again; I will not be a fool
And sex, it seems so open for everyone to explore
Three girls I know that came to school don't come here
anymore
If only I could make a difference

ACKNOWLEDGEMENTS

Public School 3

Teacher: MS. COSTAGLIOLA

Student: OMRI JOHNSON

Public School 4

Teacher: MR. Jose Cantu

Students:

ARLENE ALVARADO	RUTHANN MUNOZ
ARTURO CAMPOS	SAMANTHA LEON
BRIANI DEL OBRE	STEPHANI POLANCO
JACOB VASQUEZ	THANAYRI VERAS
KIOMI RAMOS	VICTORIA PANNEL
RACHELLE HERNANDEZ	YORLIBETH MARTINEZ

Public School 6, Region 9

Teachers:

MS. LEVENHERZ	MS. PATTY TABACCHI

Students:

ELIZABETH BAUER	BESS DANIEL
RAY FISHMAN	

ACKNOWLEDGEMENTS

Public School 18

Teachers:

MS. F. SMITH   MS. A. WILLIAMS

Student: ATAJAH WILLIAMS

Public School 19, Staten Island, Region 7

Teachers: MS. VIVIAN PORCU

Students:

ALLISON BABILONIA   RADWA ABBAS
CECILIA TOM   RUBEN SIBRI
EMANUEL LUGO   SANTOS MOLASCO
JASMIN GARCIA   SEMIR MUSOVSKI
JENNYFER GOMEZ   SOPHIA GUARINO
KALINDI MISHRA   STEPANIE JACKSON
KATHERINE CRIOLLO   TREMIKA GEORGE
LUIS EVANS   VALERIE TORRES
NICHOLAS BENEDETTO   WILLIAM FELDER

ACKNOWLEDGEMENTS

Public School 35

Teachers:

MS. KOSTER   MS. MIKHAIL

MS. RAMNARINE

Students:

ADRIAN VARGAS   MARITA AGYEPONG
ANAIS GONZALEZ   MICHAEL DAMOA
ANGEL FUENTES SANG   MIRANDALY MARTINEZ
BRIAN TAVERAS   MOHAMED BAJAHA
CARMELO BRETON   MYKEL AGYENIM
CHRIS ROSAS   NEYSSA BISSOON
DANAJAH WARREN   RACHEL ARAUZ
JUSTIN SPENCER   STEPHEN MONCRIEFFE
KIMBERLY DELGADO   TIRANKE KABA
LATOYA WHITE   YASMELY PAYANO
LYNEETH NAVARRO   YERDI TAVAREZ
MARIAMA SILLAH   YVES PASUBIDA

ACKNOWLEDGEMENTS

Public School 36, Bronx, Region 8

Teachers:

MR. ANTIGUA	MS. DILG
MS. AXELRAD	MS. LAMARUGGINE
MS. LAUREN CAHILL	MS. SPRATLEY
MR. DEVANNY	MS. ZIVAN

Students:

BRANDON TORAIN	LAUREN NAVARRO
DENNIS RAMDIN	MAEGAN TALVY
ENOC ESTEVES	MAIYA GONZALEZ
ERIKA MCGIBBON	MARGARET JACOBS
FARZANA BEGUM	NANCY MORALES
JANAE PENA	NIRMA GOLDER
JOANNA HUANG	SALEEMA MOORE
JON CERON	SANZIDA TALUKDER
LAUREN NAVARRO	

Public School 39, Region 8

Teacher: MS. PISINO

Student: RACHEL DUKE

ACKNOWLEDGEMENTS

Middle School 47

Teacher: MS. ALEXA JACKOWSKI

Student: KATHY RUGGIERO

Middle School 51, Region 8

Teacher: MS. OBERCIAN

Student: ANNA DUKE

Public School 53

Teachers:
MS. COLON   MS. GILBERT

Students:
ELIZABETH GENTILE   KARIS ISRALSKY

ACKNOWLEDGEMENTS

Public School 55, District 31

Teachers:

MR. ALVARO MS. ECOCK

Students:

ALEXANDRA WALSH MALLORY SPRINGSTEAD
STEVEN WREN

Public School 75, Region 2

Teachers:

MS. GUILLERMO MR. IMPERATI
MS. MURRAY

Students:

BRIAN RODRIGUEZ FELIPE COATL
CRYSTAL WHITE KATHERINE CORTEZ
DALIA SAAVEDRA KELVIN HERNANDEZ
DESTINEE GONZALEZ KURON WILLIAMS
ELISABETH BIKOKO LEANDRA NUNEZ

ACKNOWLEDGEMENTS

Public School 105, Region 2

Teachers:

MS. ALI
MS. BRUNKHURST

MS. VASQUEZ
MS. VOLPE

Students:

ALEX ACEVEDO
BRIANNA BRYAN-KERR
DANIEL REYES
KEVIN READ

LUCERO BRITO
MYRANDA RODRIGUEZ
NUHIRATH RAFTHIA
TAISHA LOMBA

Public School/Middle School 147, Queens

Teachers:

MS. COHEN
MS. DOWLING
MR. SIEMINSKI

Students:

ALEXANDRA JEAN-PHILIPE
ANDREA FREDERICK
BRIANNA DALEY
CHELSEA LONGMORE

CLAIRE JANVIER
MARVIN LACOMBE
MELISSA KING
NYRON SAWH

ACKNOWLEDGEMENTS

Public School 161, Region 6

Teachers:

MS. COCHRANE   MS. GOLUB
MS. COLEMAN   MR. PORTER
MS. ROSENBURG

Students:

CHASSIDY DAVID   NAGAMA KISTOO
CHAVELLE ROYER   REBEKAH WILLIAMS
CRAIG CELESTINE   RYAN COOKS
IMANI DIXON   SCHWANIQUA CUNNINGHAM
KALON MATTHEW   WITNA MICHEL
KELLY DIAZ   YAFAHAL DORNEVEIL
MADISON JEAN PHILIPPE

Public School 165, Region 5

Teachers:

MS. HUMPHREY   MS. MODESTE

Students:

ANTHONY ARNOLD   MELINA PENA
KAYA THOMAS   MORGAN ZHANE
MADAYJA TYLER   SHAQUANA JOHN

ACKNOWLEDGEMENTS

Middle School 167

Teacher: Ms. KERRY DOYLE

Student: MAX HYAMS

Public School 178, Region 3

Teacher: MS. FRIETAS

Students:
CALEB HONG   GREGORY GOODMAN
JOSHUA SIMMONS

Public School 183, District 2

Teacher: SARAH LEVINE

Students:
ALESSANDRA BALDARI   KIRAN SRIVATAVA
SAM JACOVITZ

ACKNOWLEDGEMENTS

CS 200

Students:

ADAM DIABY	JOSHUA ALLEN
ANDREANNA OGILVIE	KATHERINE VEGA
BINTOU KANE	LETY LANDEVERDE
DONOVAN JONES	LINDA DESMANGLES
ELIJAH REYNOLDS	MADELINE PERALTA
FARA BARGOURA	RYAN CHANCEY
JAMES GRANT	SARAN KANE
JARETT ALLEN	THOMAS MCNEIL
JASON NELSON	YUSUF BROWN

Public School/Middle School 207, Queens

Teachers:

MS. CLOSE   MS. FELIX

MS. ROS

Students:

NICOLE SKOLNICK   ALANA STEWART

ACKNOWLEDGEMENTS

Public School 208

Teacher: MS MUNCHEZ

Students:
AMBER HARRISON   ERICK SERRANO
DIAMOND LUMPKIN   JOARLUYN VASQUEZ
MAURAE COTTMAN

Public School 215, District 21

Teacher: MS TROPEA

Students:
CHRISTOPHER TROCHE   RESHAWYAL ABBAS
MAYA LORD DAGOSTINO

ACKNOWLEDGEMENTS

Public School 232, District 27, Queens

Teachers:

MS ARMENIA	MRS MEADE
MS BOLTITA	MS PARKER
MS GRIEG	MS STETINA

MR WALTER

Students:

ADRIAN EGO-AGUIRRE	JAN NOHACZEWSKI
ALDEN KIM	JEAN PAUL PEREZ
AMY SUKHOO	KIARA ALFARA
ANTHONY VELIZ	RACHEL SAKHAI
BRANDON OSANDO	SARAH GAFUR
CAMRYN MORALES	SEAKWON GRAHAM
CATHERINE DELEON PS	SOUFIAN RMIDI
CHRISTOPHER MOSCHITTA	STEVEN BANGIOVANNI
EMELY COLLADO	TAYLOR LOMBARDINO
GINA RINGSTON	VANESSA SANCHEZ
GLORYVEE PAULA	VINCENTO LAZO JR
HIFSA UMAR	WILLIAM ANDERSON
HUSSEIN KHOKHAR	XAVIER GUADALUPE

ZACHARY BOODOO

ACKNOWLEDGEMENTS

Public School 241

Students:

BREYENNA WATSON   KETSHELL PIERRE
DAVON OLIVE   MICHAEL ORSI
ISAAC AGUILAR   MIKA PEREIRA
JARAI JALLON   RENELLE VILLAFANA
TYMEL PATRICK

Public School 268, Region 6, District 18

Teachers:

MS HAMILTON   MS LOUIS
MS HAYNES   MS MENDEZ
MS LARSON   MS REMISE
MR LAURENT   MS WILLIAMS
MS LEWIS   MS WILSON

Students:

ALICIA FRASER   KEISHAWN BRYANT
ALLISHA ROACH   KEMROM THOMAS
ALYSSA WORTHY   KEYANNA ALLEN
ANGELICA MATTHEW   KINO CHALTENHAM
ANGELIQUE CUMMINGS   KURTIS SMITH
ANTONIA BAILEY   LUZ GOMEZ
ARIANNA LANGAIGNE   MARKENLAND LEFRANCE
ARYANNA MCFARLANE   MYA GITTENS
ASHLEY NURSE   NERMA LA FRANCE
CHENISE CHAMBERS   ORIN JOHNSON

ACKNOWLEDGEMENTS

Public School 268, Region 6, District 18

Students:

CHRISTALEE WOOLRIDGE	KAYLA MEDINA
DARREL WOODFORD	RAVENNE COOPER
DIAMOND LUCAS	SERRINA TEMPLEMAN
DONALD BERGER	SHAMAR POWELL
GABRIELLE FORD	SHAQUILLA MORRIS
GIVAN OSORIO	SUKARI WEBB
JADA ALLISON	TAJEET SINGH
JAIDEN THOMPSON	TAKEISHA CASIMIR
JAMAAL WRITE	TALIAH VINCENT
JAMAL BRYAN	TYRA PHILLIP
JELANI HARRY	VICTORIA LEWIS
JENNASIA OTWAY	WEKESHA POWELL
JENNIFER SMITH	XAVIER SMITH
KAYLA BERNARD	ZAYNEB MOSLEH

ZURI GIBBS

ACKNOWLEDGEMENTS

Public School 277, Region 6

Teacher: MS. RAPHAEL

Students:

ASHLEY EATON	KRISTEN DALY
CAROLYN HAYES	MADISON FERNANDEZ
CORRAL RUSSO	MANSSA MORAN

Other

Teachers:

Ms. NIVIA MALDANADO   MS. MURPHY

Students:

ASHONTINIQ WOODS	SELAH SANSCULOTTE
MICHAEL GRIMA	ZHANE MORGAN

THE COMMUNITY BOOK STORE

All of us here at the Community Book Store would like to thank all of you for making our annual poetry contest such a success.

Also, thank you to all of the parents, teachers, parent coordinators, principals and other school staff for their support and for getting their children and schools involved in this creative endeavor.

We enjoyed reading each of the poems submitted by all these talented individuals and can definitively say that the children of New York City has a lot to offer.

Lastly, as a reminder, the previous editions of the Children of NYC: Straight from the Heart are available for purchase via the below order form or by contacting us.

Very truly yours,

Natalie McKenzie
Owner

THE CHILDREN OF NYC: STRAIGHT FROM THE HEART
- $14.95 each or 2 copies for $20.00 – can mix and match.
  (Include NYC 8.375% tax when submitting your order or submit tax exempt letter)

Support your children and order a copy today!

2006 Edition: Quantity: _____   Amount Enclosed: _____

2005 Edition: Quantity: _____   Amount Enclosed: _____

2004 Edition: Quantity: _____   Amount Enclosed: _____

Send check or money order (please no cash) to:

The Community Book Store
Attn: Ms. Mckenzie
156 Hancock Street Apt. 1
Brooklyn, NY 11216

*Any questions or concerns will be answered by **Calling: (718) 638-2218**- Leave a detailed message OR send us an **Email at: thecommunitybookstore@yahoo.com**
Checks and/or money orders should be made payable to: The Community Book Store

Printed in the United States
By Bookmasters